# HOW TO BUILD A STRONG BLACK MAN

Marvin O'Bryant

*How to Build a Strong Black Man*
© 2020 Marvin O'Bryant

ISBN: 978-1-7350965-0-6

All rights reserved

All rights reserved. No part of this publication may be reproduced, distributed, or transmitted in any form or by any means, including
photocopying, recording, or other electronic or mechanical methods without the prior written permission of the publisher, except in the case of brief quotation embodied in critical reviews and certain other non-commercial uses permitted by copyright law.

For permission requests, email the publisher, addressed: "Attention Permission Coordinator," at the following address:

Samone Publishing
Drsamone2016@gmail.com

samonepublishing.com

# DEDICATION

*I dedicate this book to Mrs. Walker, my seventh grade
English teacher at Southeast Junior High
in Pine Bluff, Arkansas.
She inspired me to not give up on my writing.
My writing impressed her,
and that stuck with me for years.*

*I also dedicate it to the black men who grew up without a
clue or role model to know or see what
a strong black man looks like.*

*Finally, I dedicate it to the black men I have
encountered: uncles, cousins, coaches, educators, preachers,
business owners, entrepreneurs,
professionals, and other positive men.*

# CONTENTS

| | |
|---|---|
| INTRODUCTION | 1 |
| CHAPTER 1<br>UNDERSTANDING PURPOSE | 7 |
| CHAPTER 2<br>THE INGREDIENTS | 13 |
| CHAPTER 3<br>MESSAGES TO MY SISTERS AND BROTHERS | 45 |

# Introduction

I have poured my heart and soul into this book and I thank you for giving me the opportunity to share my 52 years of wisdom, knowledge, and life experiences. I have been a barber for at least 30 years. Day after day of standing behind the barber chair, I have experienced men and women, grandparents, great grandparents, aunts and uncles, who brought in young men who were totally lost or lacked wisdom, ambition, and drive.

Many people enter the barbershop adorned with cell phones, video games, and Jordan tennis shoes. Rarely do they interact with each other and the majority of the time, they don't have a clue concerning what kind of haircut or style they want. When I was a child, it was an honor to go with my granddad, Johnny O'Bryant, or my brothers, cousins, and uncles to Miller's Barbershop by the lake or BNS, back in Pine Bluff, Arkansas. I quietly sat and listened to the stories and jokes that were told by the customers as they waited. I received much needed wisdom and knowledge.

Times have changed. We are distracted by the things of the world. Almost no one shares their knowledge. Today's conversation, if any, take place against the backdrop of loud music and is different and difficult.

I wrote this book because of my care and concern. I care about our today's men and the men of the next generation. I admit I don't know everything. I do know a little bit about a lot of subjects. Even though I looked and listened a lot, I still made mistakes.

The first book I wrote was, *Life Without a Father.* It detailed how I went without a lot of understanding, comprehension, and the push a young man needs to go forward. I bumped my head many times. I thought I had the answers and I knew it all. As many people have said, "A hard head makes a soft behind."

Many of today's women think a young man doesn't necessarily need a male or a father-figure in his life. They do. He needs to have a hero in his life. Heroines have their place, but a boy needs a male to be there with him and for him, step by step. I can only explain it like this: We love to make our moms proud, but it is another feeling when there's a male figure available to support and push us as young man to handle manly agendas. For example, how to handle business at an early age, how to count money, how to write a check, how to properly use a credit or debit card, or even how to use a laptop computer. Now these items are asexual and can be taught by a woman, however the learning experience will serve a young boy well when taught by a male.

This book can't make you a man, but it can encourage you to be a strong black man. Anyone who has known me over these last 52 years knows I am not prejudiced and I do not have a racist bone in my body. I love everybody, but at this period in my life, I look at my race of black men and I feel we lack male responsibilities. I will be the first to raise my hand and testify that I am now a strong black man. However, it took failure and disappointment to make me think, smarten up, and pay attention to what it means to be a strong black man.

Building a strong black man starts from the womb, not three, five, or ten years later. A black man needs to hear a man's voice early in life, and he will grow up to respect that tone of voice. If there isn't any respect or reverent fear almost from day one, catastrophic mistakes and failures will most likely follow.

I grew up in North Little Rock, Arkansas. People there called it Dark Hollow because there were no streetlights in the black community. My great grandparents, Lucy and John Shelton, raised me. We lived at 811 E. 16th Street. It was an honor because they gave me the foundation of upright morals, respect, responsibility, and a good work ethic. They taught me how to dig a garden, make rows, and plant seeds when I was seven. I also shelled peas, picked beans, and hung clothes on the clothesline. I watched my great grandfather build birdhouses, and fix up the house. I learned structure. When we went to the grocery store, I learned to say, "Yes sir," "No sir," "Yes ma'am," and "No ma'am." In church, I learned that it was okay to shake the preacher's hand after the sermon. I also learned the hard way that you do not talk when grown folks have a conversation.

For example, once, my great grandmother talked to our next-door neighbor, Ms. Velma, about the price of tomatoes at the grocery store. She told Ms. Velma that the price of those tomatoes was $2 and I stepped in and said, "No they are not. They are $1.50."

Immediately, I got back-handed and I never made that mistake again. Needless to say, I was disciplined when needed. You cannot spare the rod because if you do, you will spoil the child.

The most important lesson I learned from my great grandparents was how to pay attention to detail. I watched them make a garden from scratch. They took a shovel and turned the dirt; took a hoe and chopped up the dirt, made a straight row, then planted the seeds. They watered the seeds daily. This is the same way you raise a young boy. You cannot miss a day because if you do, you will delay his growth.

I became an entrepreneur at the age of nine, because my great grandfather taught me how to cut a yard with a little red and white lawn mower. He told me if I wanted to make money, I could cut other people yards for ten dollars.

I asked him, "How do you that?"

He said, "Easy, you knock on the doors of people with high grass and ask them, 'Can I cut your yard?'

When they ask, how much?' Tell them ten dollars, front and back."

That day, I cut three yards and made thirty dollars. I was amazed and happy and could not wait to start my day the next morning. A highway separated the black and white neighborhoods. I pushed my lawn mower to the gas station, and bought twenty-five cents worth of gas to put in my gas can. I cut five yards in the white neighborhood. By twelve noon, I had made fifty dollars. When I returned home, my great grandmother had made fried chicken, black-eyed peas, macaroni and cheese, and cornbread. I ate, took a nap, got up, and cut five more yards on my side of town. They were my my Uncle Richard, my Aunt Edna, Preacher Mathis, Ms. Maeola, and Ms. Georgia. I made $100 in one day. Not bad for a nine-year-old. I knew then, I would be somebody in life.

My great grandmother taught me a valuable lesson, when it comes to giving back. She woke me up early the next morning to go and cut the yard of her friend, Ms. Narvell Aycocks. I cut her yard, but she did not pay me and I left mad. I pushed my lawn mower, MAD, put it up, MAD, and went to my room, MAD. My great grandmother called me back down to the kitchen and when I got there, there was a cake and twenty dollars.

I asked, "What is this for?"

She told me, "Sometimes it is best to do something for others because you might wind up getting more."

In other words, do what is right because you may never know which way or from whom your blessings will come from.

My brothers and sisters, the Bible says, "Train up a child in the way that it should go: and when he is old, he will not depart from it" (Proverbs 22:6). This is the start of the ingredients I will give you in this book. There will come a time when a young man will do what he wants to do, but he won't be able to say he didn't know better. For instance, once I made a mistake when I rode my bike to school. I didn't lock it when I parked it. When I was ready to go home, I discovered my bike had been stolen. I walked home.

When I made it home, my great grandmother asked, "Where is your bike?"

"Stolen."

"Did you lock it?"

"No."

"Now you knew better than that."

I stood there and looked foolish, but I could not be mad at anybody but myself.

*Welcome to the ingredients of how to build a strong black man.*

# Chapter 1

# Understanding Purpose

We all have a purpose in life. We must find out what that purpose is. Building a strong black man starts with strong black men who strengthened weaker black boys with wisdom and knowledge about what made them strong. These are my ingredients. The ingredients by themselves do not sound good. Here is an example. The other day, my wife set out flour, eggs, sugar, cinnamon, and nutmeg for a cake. I thought to myself, *that doesn't look good.*

I watched her as she mixed the ingredients together and put them in the oven. The object that came out looked good and smelled good. I almost ate the whole cake by myself. In review, when my wife started to make the cake, the ingredients in the bowl did not look good to me, but she placed the pan in the oven and put the oven on the right temperature. She went back from time to time to check it, and to my surprise, it turned out to be a beautiful, light brown, tasty pound cake.

Looks are deceiving. We can line up one hundred young black boys and there wouldn't be a way to tell what any of them would be when they become a man.

The ingredients we put in them to prepare them to become a strong black man makes a difference.

I wrote my previous book, *Life without a Father* because as a young boy, I needed attention every day. When I did not receive it, I became angry, rebellious, and unhappy. I did what old folks said, I "smelled" myself. I did not want to do what I was told by my mother who wasn't around much, or my grandmother who raised me. I did not want to listen to anybody, and I was angry at the world. I was a walking time bomb—ready to explode. I saw and felt the gap where the females in my life, did not have any input in me being a man. I finally learned to listen to older men at a young age. Those men filled the gap of manhood that I desperately needed. There were many of them. When I saw two or three older men talking, I would ease up on my bike to eavesdrop on their conversation. I am full of wisdom and knowledge because of the older men I crossed paths with as a young boy.

My brothers, if you have children, and more directly, sons, please make sure you spend quality time with them. Do not rob them of the ingredient of their father being in their lives. You need to be present, daily. The ingredients are not only for material things or phone calls. You need to be there regardless of the relationship between you and their mother or other family members. At the end of the day, your absence isn't any different from a missing ingredient in a cake.

Can you imagine eating a cake that did not have eggs, butter, or sugar?

I have heard many young boys say, "I don't know where my daddy is," "my daddy is in jail," "my daddy is dead," or "my daddy is on drugs." It hurts me to imagine what goes on in their hearts and minds. Do not get me wrong. I understand many children are born in this world out of wedlock, but there is still an obligation to that child; not for you, but for his sake.

I was married with a son, but separated from his mother early in his life. She moved all over before coming back to Arkansas, then to California, and finally, Texas. I found myself thinking *how I am going to get to Arkansas, California, or Texas on a regular basis?* I was only able to see my son two to three times a year. That is not good because when I saw him, my absence showed. I saw him in an unhappy state. He didn't want to talk and his feelings were balled up inside of him. He went through the motions and moped around. It was a sad time for us.

Parents do not understand that children will hide their feelings for as many years as they need to do so. Some may hide as many as 52 years in some cases, if you catch my drift, and others a lifetime. If your relationship should end in a break up, do not let it turn bitter to the point where your son hears you talk negatively about each other. It does not need to be ugly and can be a cancer to a young man's mind, body, and soul. By the same token, many women scandalize the father's name by saying, "he is being a low down dirty dog," and keep their children away from him, whether he pay child support or not. They don't understand this hurts the family. Now, there is a double hurt. Two wrongs don't make a right and at the end of the day, when the father and mother enter into another relationship, the son is left to deal with his feelings on his own.

In my situation, if I only knew how much my actions then, would affect so much now. If I could turn back the hands of time, I would have done some things differently. This is a pain I would not wish on anybody because once children get grown, they get gone. They take the hurt with them and distance themselves. Parents, when you break up, if your son gets any information at all, he needs both sides of the story. Clearly the story must be appropriate, but it must be fair and balanced. If not, he is a car riding on a flat tire — tilted to one side. Teach him to love each parent in spite of the breakup.

Many times young mothers bring their sons to the barbershop, and for the most part, the boys seemingly have no life in them, no drive, and no hope. There are many pieces missing to the puzzle of some of their lives.

As a barber for over 30 years, many women have clung to me. They wanted my phone number only to talk about how to raise their sons. They saw my concern and they saw the interest their sons had in me. Some mothers called and said their five-year-old sons wanted to come back and see me. What I missed as a child, I wanted to give to them and it worked. It happened again recently.

I mentored a young man some 20 years ago when he came in to get his hair cut. He got into a lot of mischief and gave his mom a lot of trouble. He reminded me of myself, and plus, I liked his personality. They struggled financially and they lived at the Pebble Creek Apartments. I "adopted" him and cut his hair free of charge. I gave him money to get something to eat from time to time. He's about 30 now. I was at a gas station and I ran into him and his girlfriend. We embraced tightly and he introduced me as his "pops." He did not know it, but I had to turn away before he could see the tears in my eyes. I did not know he thought of me in that way.

I thank God at this moment for my years of being a barber, but not only as someone who cuts hair. I thank Him for the opportunity to share wisdom, love, and knowledge to those who needed it, especially the young boys. I encourage every barber around the world to pay close attention to their young male clients. If you look at their facial expressions and their body languages, you will be able to tell something is wrong or missing. They will open up to you one haircut at a time. Get to know them on a first name basis. A young boy loves that you know his name, and that you called his name when he entered the barbershop. If you say, "What's up, Greg?" you will often see the biggest smile on his face. I have seen it a thousand times.

We only get one mother and one father. Our mother will, for the most part, nourish us and love us in spite of what we do and become. She birthed us, and will never stop loving us until the day she dies. She can only give us what a woman can give and that is her love.

On the other hand, our father is more of a hardcore lover. Often men have a different way of showing love. He may not say the words, "I love you," and we may never get a kiss on the cheek, or a hug from him. However he is designed to provide for and protect us.

## Chapter 2

## The Ingredients

**Put God First**

The black man should know who God is. He is the creator of the whole universe. God created everything, the heavens and the earth and He said, "It is good." Everything a young black man will need, God put at his disposal. However, he needs to learn it as a boy. Help him learn to pray early in life. Start with how to pray over food at the table. A young man must get to know God for himself through praying daily, morning, noon, and night, and praying for what he wants and needs. He must pray for others—family members and friends. He also needs to know when all else fails, he can go to God in prayer.

**Love**

Love by definition is, *a deep affection or intense feeling, or to take great interest in*. God says "love thy neighbor," which means it does not matter what creed, color, or race you are, we are to love unconditionally. It is important to understand what love is. It is not only your words, but also your actions.

## Respect

Respect everyone at all times, especially your elders. When you greet a man, whether he's young or older, first start with a firm handshake and look him straight in the eye, and introduce yourself. For example, "Hello, my name is George Brown. How are you doing today?" Answer with, "Yes sir," or "no sir," when talking to a man, and when talking to a woman, your response should be, "Yes ma'am, no ma'am."

Now, I realize that's more of a southern thing, and some people call it "slave language." I call it respect. At the least, your language with grown-ups should be different from your peers.

## Smile

It is always great to smile when you encounter someone. A smile immediately lets them know you are physically and mentally okay and that you are in a good mood. A simple smile can disarm many situations and can keep people from jumping to conclusions about your mood or your attitude.

## Attitude

Your attitude has much to do with how a person receives you, which means you cannot let something you are upset about, spill onto someone else. They do not deserve it. Do not be bitter, hateful, disrespectful, or stubborn, to name a few. Negative attitudes like these can destroy relationships, both now and in the future.

## Responsibilities

Mothers and fathers, teach your children to be responsible at an early age. When you give them responsibilities, set the expectations they need to be carried out at an appointed time, not when they are ready to do them. Cut the yard, today; do your homework, today; take a bath, today. Do not leave room for assumptions about what should be done and how it should be carried out.

## Discipline

This transcends race, but if you want your child to respect you, discipline starts at birth. If you do not discipline him, he will develop his own way of thinking and will want to do things his way. He needs to understand life is not like the old Burger King slogan. One cannot always "have it your way" or behave the way you want to.

Parents should set a time to eat, a time to wake up, a time to go to bed, and a time for play. If you keep this pattern, he will know from a young age, there is discipline in all areas of life. It is also important that physical discipline come into play. My great grandmother did not whip me often. She would look at me, and I knew what that look meant and that was punishment enough. My grandfather, Johnny O'Bryant, on the other hand would say, "Go get me a switch" or he would pull his belt off and apply corporal punishment on the spot. That was his way of disciplining me. My mother, "Kitty," would whip me with a conversation first.

She would ask something like, "Didn't I tell you to wash dishes?"

"Yes ma'am."

Then I would get a whipping with either a switch, extension cord, house shoe, dishrag, or belt to name a few. I do realize corporal punishment exists mainly in southern states. There's only a couple of western states that allow some form of corporal punishment. Fifty-six nations have banned corporal punishment. Another 55 nations have made progress towards the goal of banning violence against children both in school and in the home. The bottom line is however you mete out discipline, there should be consequences for his actions.

Allow me to acknowledge my mother, my queen, my superwoman. When I was in her care, she protected us from all harm and danger like a mother hen. She did not let anybody babysit us at anytime. She made sure we were well-sheltered and well-fed at all times. I have never went hungry and I never went without what I needed. I might not have always got what I wanted and that is fine now. I have come to realize that a young boy does not need everything he wants. That is ridiculous. Even though he may throw a tantrum or cry because he does not get everything he wants, it is okay. It is called "growing pains" and he will get over it. My mother did not play that, especially when we went into a store and I saw something I wanted and she said no. I dare not fall out on the floor, or start crying because if I did, she dealt with me right there on the spot. She did not wait until we got home.

**Anger**

Sometimes I was not allowed to go outside to play or I could not talk on the phone, or watch television. It made me frustrated and when I could not do anything about it, it made me angry. Anger came into my life and it will come into any other young boy's life. It is okay to be disappointed or upset, but not angry. Anger can open the door to violence. Teach a young boy how to manage his anger and frustration to not take it out on friends, classmates, and siblings, and in some cases, pets. Another potential risk is as he gets older, there is a possibility he could take it out on you. You do not want to lead your child into being argumentative and defensive. That is a no-no. You want to shut those possibilities down quickly by taking control of the situation.

Frustration can also be horrible when he cannot fix it. For instance, he asks "Why not?"

"Because I said so!" you answer.

He is frustrated because you did not fix it or he cannot fix it and now it could lead to violence such as throwing things, having tantrums, and slamming doors. Although I am a proponent of corporal punishment, I do know violence begets violence. Often he mimics the corporal punishment he received. He doesn't have a child to whip, but he whips whatever he throws, he whips himself by tantrums, and he whips doors when he slams them.

My son used to throw gaming remote controls when he was frustrated about losing. I am also guilty. I called my grandparents to "tell on" my mother. I would let them know what she didn't do, what she didn't buy me, or the reason she disciplined me. I called out of frustration.

**Patience**

We must teach our young boys how to be patient. Hardly anyone wants to get to know patience, but we must systematically teach them that patience is necessary. The old saying goes, "Patience is a virtue." When I went to Pine Bluff in the tenth grade, I played second-string linebacker for the Zebras. Tiger Henderson was a senior who started at linebacker ahead of me. I felt I was as good as he, but I knew the coaches would start him. I knew I was bigger, faster, stronger, and could tackle as hard as he could. If I wanted to play, however, I needed patience. By the fifth game, I started because Tiger went out with a pinched nerve injury in his shoulder. It was now my time. I patiently waited for it.

Along those lines, a young ordained minister may be called to pastor his own church, but it takes patience before he may be ready to take on that challenge.

A young boy may want his own car, but it takes patience before he is ready to handle the responsibility.

A new attorney may have recently passed the bar, but that does not mean he gets a position with a firm tomorrow. It takes patience and preparation to get to that step.

**Education**

Boys need to know how to spell, read, write, and speak. This should happen before pre-school or kindergarten. Those subjects are more important than how to play the latest electronic game. I did not get motivated by education until the tenth grade. That's when I found out I was being recruited to play football and I could earn a scholarship. Previously, I went to school to have fun, play sports, flirt, dress nice, and look good. My big goal was to play college and professional sports, but my lifetime goal was to be one of the best criminal attorneys in the world. Had I focused more on my education I probably could have passed the bar with flying colors. Education needs to be a priority to a young boy.

## Scholarships

Black people are the most talented and gifted people on the earth. Our young men yearn to show us their skills and their brilliance in the classroom, on the stage, or on the athletic field. They want to maximize their potential. We must get this machine running. Let him get involved, turn him loose, and let him fly.

One of the saddest things that happens to little boys is that parents let them go through 12 years of school and get ready for graduation, but when they are asked what they want to do, their reply is, "I don't know, " or "I am still thinking about it." They don't know what college or university they want to attend, what they want to major in, or even if they want to go. How do you raise a child and they not know? Do not waste time. Start them to thinking early about higher education and their career. Do not cross this road. There are too many scholarship opportunities our sons should take advantage of. People are giving away money. No one should have to pay for higher education because our sons are too competitive in the classroom, and on the field. There is no reason for our young men to only choose between the top schools among the Historically Black Colleges and Universities, and not schools like Harvard, Yale, Cornell, or Duke.

They should also have a Plan A, B, or C, because it may not work out the way they want it to. Instead of settling for one skill, let them work on multiple skillsets in order to have options for success. Meanwhile, help them stay focused and to not get caught up in high school relationships—girls or people in general. Distractions can delay progress. Keep them focused on the prize and let them know they have plenty of time for love. I went to Oklahoma University on a football scholarship and because I was in love, I left before the season started to attend the University of Central Arkansas in Conway, Arkansas. I wanted to be closer to my girlfriend, but that was not close enough. I eventually transferred to the University of Arkansas at Pine Bluff. Nothing worked out for me there. She became pregnant and I wound up going to barber school. Now being a barber has been good to me, but I let go of my dream of being a criminal attorney. My point is, be careful of strong relationships at a young age.

**Laziness**

Do not let your son be lazy or hang around lazy people. Laziness is cancerous to a young boy. Your son is lazy when he chooses to stay up late at night to play games, talk on the phone, fall asleep in class, not do assigned chores or when he always have an excuse. Laziness opens the door for procrastination. Do not fall to laziness and procrastination with your sons.

**Right and Wrong**

Teach your son the difference between right and wrong. Teach him that right will always defeat wrong such as when it comes to lying or cheating. Neither of those will get anyone out of trouble. Always tell the truth. More often than not, a lie will catch up with the liar. The best example of this is by the way you live your life. Know your son is watching you, even when you think he isn't.

**Gifts and Talents**

At an early age, pay close attention to your son, because God has instilled gifts and talents in him. It could be sports, singing, dancing, music, painting, crafting or building, writing, cooking, or even the care of animals. Find out what the gift or talent is and give guidance concerning how to develop the skill-set. Make your son practice, because practice makes perfect. That same little boy will thank you and make you proud. Why? Because you found out his gift and made him practice to be the best he could be.

**Motivation**

Another key component is motivation tied to their gifts and talents. For example, it is okay to take children to concerts to hear professional singers and musicians. Take them to art festivals and exhibits to see artists' artwork. If they want to be an attorney, police officer, or a firefighter, take them to meet professionals in those categories, but at some point, they must go from being spectators to being active participators. This will allow them to live their best and be able to give back to others.

**Sports**

I believe sports is important to a young man's life. From sports he learns teamwork, discipline, competition, brotherhood, mental toughness, stamina, and overall physical health. These lessons will carry him far in his adult life. When women raise sons who participate in sports, they get additional encouraging support from coaches, other dads, grandparents, uncles, and big brothers. In other words, you do not have to do it alone.

For example, when I played Little League Football, I was bitter, angry, and frustrated, but my coaches, Ed Johnson, and the two twins from Little Rock, Arkansas, filled the gap from my missing father. They replaced my emotional turmoil with slaps on the helmet, and a pat on the bottom (when it was acceptable). When I received these congratulations, they gave me a good feeling and a determination to keep that good feeling going. It continued into my middle school and high school years and kept me away from the trouble that came with such things as drugs and violence. When I participated in sports, I had men in my life I did not want to disappoint. I still say it takes a village to raise a child.

## Failure

A young boy will attempt to break boundaries, especially, if he does not have a father. It is natural for a child to be curious, touch items, pick up and break belongings because he misses something, although he is in search of it. He will fail at many things, but failure is okay as long as he learns something and immediately gets back up. Failure among other things, builds character, motivation, execution, determination, stamina, practice, and eventually, it builds success.

## Friends

I believe most of us will have three best friends in life: a childhood friend, a college friend, and a friend developed professionally or in church (religious affiliation). I also believe it is possible to find a friend in a parent, sibling, or relative. One of my best friends, Reginald Adams from Pine Bluff, Arkansas, told me "friendship is nothing but a relationship."

In other words, a friendship isn't any different from a marriage. One must like being around their friend, like their style, like their conversation, and have mutual respect and concern for them. A friend must have a listening ear, especially in the time of need. That means a friend must often stop what he (or she) is in the middle of to see about you. In return, will you do the same?

**Respectful**

I thank God once again for my upbringing, ranging from my grandparents to my "village." I learned much about being respectful, therefore it irks me when I see a young boy or young man being disrespectful, especially in public. When I observe this type of behavior, I think, *who are his parents?*

**Sex**

I cannot stress enough to be careful, and practice safe sex. It is important to wait until you are ready physically, spiritually, and emotionally, before you bring a child into the world. Mothers, let your son spend time with his father, his uncles, and grandfathers. If you are a single parent, do not hesitate to ask for help. I have a son and daughter out of wedlock that I did not acknowledge until they were grown. One of them I did not know existed until she was nineteen. I see how my mistakes have affected our lives by the hurt they and I feel. Can it be fixed? My daughter will not speak to me, but she will let me see the grandchildren. My oldest son does not think I care, and I have not spoken to my youngest son in three years.

## Listening

Another good ingredient is listening and being able to express yourself. Make sure you have a good understanding. It is a lost art. Most of the time our definition of listening is waiting long enough to respond, whether it is appropriate or inappropriate (Stephen R. Covey). When we engage in listening, a greater understanding and learning take place and we are better equipped to handle whatever situation arises. It's been said, "That's why the good Lord gave us two ears and one mouth." We can listen more and talk less.

## Time

Time waits for no one. That is profound. Our sons need to know time and timing is everything. We must also teach them time is important. I too, had to learn time is of the essence when it comes to jobs, relationships, and business. I learned this even as barber. When clients set appointments, they expect you to be there and be prompt because you do not know what they have to do. Time is an agreement, or an appointment, and it is business. People are late for their weddings, job interviews, flights, and doctor's appointments. Back in the day, men wore watches. They wore them not only to be aware of the time of day, but to help keep them on schedule. Of course, that was before cell phones.

## Entrepreneurship

Teach your young black boy how to be an entrepreneur. He needs to know how to start his own business; whether it is washing your car every week, or cutting a yard to learn how to cut other yards. Teach him to open his own lemonade stand. One day he can own land, buy a house, and not rent a place to live for 25 to 30 years.

## Getting a Job

Parents should ask questions that people in charge of hiring will most likely ask in an interview. These questions may include: "What hours can you work?" "Are you a hard worker?" "Will you work overtime if needed?" "How can you help this company?" Make him practice with you or role-play with him. This will get him ready to participate in a proper interview. Teach him how to dress for the interview. Let him know why *you* work. Your reasons may be to take care of yourself when nobody else will, or it could be to have money in your pocket to buy the items you need and sometimes indulge your wants. You also want to prepare him to provide for his own family. My grandfather always said, "If you don't work, you will steal," and the Bible says "For even when we were with you, this we commanded you, that if any would not work, neither should he eat" (2 Thessalonians 3:10). I have found all of this to be true. Listen, if you buy your son everything he wants or needs, he will depend on you to do everything for him. If you are not careful, when you decide not to do it, he will look to other people to do it for him. Yes, he will want others to buy him a car, get his clothes, or pay for his haircuts. I call this "the parents' fault."

**Parents' Fault**

Parents should not give to the point it hinders their son's independence. He will depend on you the rest of his life. It will come back to embarrass you and his friends, girlfriend, everyone, will blame you. For example, you may think it is loving for you to fix his plate, bring his drinks to him, and clean the tub for him. He will never know how to stand on his own, and he will be crippled and handicapped, simply because he wants people to continue to do everything for him.

**Hard Work**

Show him by being an example that hard work pays off. When you get up and go to work every day, that shows how people earn money to pay their bills, put a roof over their heads, and clothes on their backs.

**Being Proud**

A sense of pride is important to a young boy. When he makes a good grade, or receive other academics achievements, let him know you are proud. When he scores a touchdown or makes a shot that helps the team, let him know you are proud. When he dresses nice, washes his face, brushes his teeth, combs his hair, or does his chores around the house, especially without asking him to do so, let him know you are proud. Do not miss this lesson.

You must also do things to make your children proud of you. You too, can put on a nice outfit, fix yourself up, and clean your car. Do not date deadbeats no matter how cool they appear. Cool does not pay bills and it sends the wrong message to your son about how he should conduct himself as an adult.

## Principles

In order for your son to have principles, you must have principles. In order for him to receive them, he must know you will stand by your principles even after he is gone and grown. Some principles include putting God first in everything you do. Other principles may be:

1. Going to church on Sunday
2. Cleaning up after yourself
3. Keeping good hygiene
4. Not using profanity
5. Obeying all house rules when you are gone
6. Being trustworthy and reliable
7. Telling the truth

**Respect the law at all Times**

Police departments across the country and around the world target young black men. Unfortunately a high percentage of the time, we are not correct on our business. We drive vehicles without insurance, our driver's license may be suspended, and we might have outstanding warrants. Some possess marijuana or other drugs and/or alcohol may be present. Chances are, you will be pulled over for simply riding three to four deep. Although this is directed to young people, the police do not care about your age. Even at my age, I have been pulled over. When you are pulled over for any reason, make sure you cooperate with the authorities. Give them what is asked for. If you do not have it, be truthful. Do not lie. Often, the police will let you go with a warning, but in case they don't, be cooperative. The goal is to get you home safely to make a report if necessary. A report is useless if you are dead.

**A Product of Your Environment**

Children are impressionable and they imitate what they see. That's why what you say, and what you do, or how you act, will be mimicked. A child hears and sees what you do from day one. If you curse, most likely, he will too. If you smoke cigarettes, he will possibly smoke your cigarettes. If you drink a lot of alcohol, he will most likely drink from your bottle. If you hit women or are otherwise abusive towards them, he will most likely do the same. If you cheat, lie, or steal, chances are good he will take on these characteristics as well. If you justifiably go to prison and are not repentant or rehabilitated, he will think nothing is wrong with life behind bars. This also works in reverse. In other words, don't let the environment ruin him, but instead let the environment be an incubator of positivity, creativity, and healthy stimulation.

**Don't Stress**

Trouble (often defined as difficulty or problems) will come to you, which means you will meet people who don't mean you any good. There's a saying, "Don't trouble trouble, until trouble troubles you." That basically means, if you believe something might cause trouble, leave it alone. People will come to you as wolves dressed in sheep's clothing. They, like Satan, come to kill, steal, and destroy according to the Bible in John 10:10.

People are often jealous and as old people say, "Nothing but the devil." They will do anything to get close to you to get what you have or to tear your success down. They will smile in your face and talk about you behind your back. Those people are called "back stabbers." They will use you although they don't even like you. I have had people whom I thought were friends, to ride around with me all day long, only to find out they couldn't stand me. Some friends have spent the night with me and stole my clothes. Others hung around me close enough to get next to my girlfriend. Often, you will find yourself in the middle of a "he said/she said" situation and you don't know anything about the ones who said anything. This is pure trouble. Help your son prepare for these possibilities to get him ready for a suitable defense. In the words of a wise friend, "Stay ready so you don't have to get ready."

**Plan and set Goals**

It is important to plan and set goals. Ask your son, "What do you want to be when you grow up?" "Where do you want to go?" "Who do you want to meet?" Help him set goals and take him on vacations away from his normal setting. Help them accomplish their goals and support them in every way possible. Let them know it is okay to dream, because dreams do come true.

**Girls and Women**

A young boy needs to know there is a difference between boys and girls. Boys are usually stronger than girls, therefore it is not okay for a boy to hit a girl. A boy should discourage girls from fighting one another. To be sure, it is not okay for boys to hit boys, but it is acceptable by society. Teach him there isn't any ugly girls because beauty comes from within. Let him know it is okay to like girls, but not all girls will like him. He can have girls as friends and as study partners. His high school girlfriend may not be his wife. Most of the time, couples marry after meeting in college or after they complete their education. Help him focus on himself and accomplish his goals because a woman needs a man who is able to stand on his own two feet.

Divorces often happen because the man does not come to the relationship with assets, a job, or stability. Women often bring more to the table from an asset standpoint. My great grandfather worked and paid the mortgage and other bills, therefore he was "in charge." Those days are gone. For a variety of reasons, many households endure a power struggle between the man and woman.

**Talk to His Pastor**

It is okay for him to go and talk to his pastor (or spiritual advisor) when there are things he might not want to discuss with family members. According to the Pew Research Center only 39 percent of Americans go to church on a regular basis. Therefore, a young boy should talk to whatever spiritual leader he has or whomever he considers to be a mentor.

**Never Give Up**

One of the best lessons you can teach a young boy is don't be a quitter. He needs to finish what he starts. If he is losing a race, tell him don't quit, finish the race. If something happens and he doesn't finish high school, he can go back and finish it. If a young lady turns him down, tell him don't quit, and suggest that he asks someone else. Again, when one door closes, another one will open.

## Chances and Challenges

Don't be afraid to take a chance and don't be afraid to step to a challenge. Life is fun when you take challenges.

When I was a young boy, I loved to be challenged. I also loved it when someone told me what I could not do. For instance, when someone said they could ride their bike faster than me or they could outrun me. It gave me energy and boosted my ego. I also loved it when someone told me I could not have *her*. Challenges are good. They feed the soul and they build character.

## Be Different

Be different, dress different, and walk different. Brand yourself. Create your own image and style. Make people remember you for being you. You do not have to act like anyone else. Chances are good, someone wants to be like you. You may not know it yet.

## Eating Healthy

From an early age, a young boy needs to know how to eat right. The black race is plagued with health conditions like high blood pressure, diabetes, poor circulation, and heart disease, due mostly to our poor eating habits. Explain to him why we don't *need* those sweets and chips. I went from 230 pounds in high school to 365 pounds. The weight is easy to put on, but it is extremely hard to take off. I am now diabetic and I take medication. I know the importance of exercise. It is not too late, but it will take some work.

**Fraternities**

I love fraternities. It does not matter what fraternity it is, I love it. If I had to pledge a fraternity, I would be an Omega Psi Phi, I love the power, the way they step with authority, the movement, the brotherhood, the support, and the love of the Omegas. I don't have anything against the pretty boys, the cool Kappas, and definitely not the Alphas, the Sigmas, and the band fraternity "KKPsi." They can all get it done. What makes them special is that it is not about rivalry, but it is about getting in where you fit in with either of these organizations. I thank all of the founders. Can you imagine what college life would be like without these fraternities? They have made many broken men—whole again. That has happened across the nation by giving them brotherhood, employment, a shoulder to cry on, and by helping them feel special or important. These brothers take those Greek letters seriously. Parents, encourage your sons to be a part of a fraternity. Take him to Greek shows to let him see what they are all about. Greek life on college campuses provide a strong foundation for peer interaction. Greek organizations build beneficial networks for students ranging from internships, referrals, and employment.

**Interracial/Biracial Sons**

I feel sorry for my young biracial brothers, but at the same time, I know what they need and want. They too, want to be loved. My biracial friends are all the same. They know they look differently, but they want to know where do they fit in? That's a hard place to be in. Most of them are angry, walking time bombs.

I was sitting at a 24 Hour Fitness center one day. I discussed the book I was writing with a friend. Seated next to me was a man who happened to overhear my conversation. He waited until I got off of the phone and said, "Excuse me sir, I wasn't trying to eavesdrop on your conversation, but did you say you are writing a book?"

I said, "Yes. It is called, *Life without a Father*."

He said, "Wow. I want to learn how to write a book, but I don't know where to start."

I asked, "What is your story?"

He told me his wife is Hispanic and from Amarillo, Texas, and he is a black man from Jackson, Mississippi. "We have two boys. When we go visit her family, our sons are usually left alone and are not accustomed to the food Grandma serves such as beans, rice, and enchiladas. When they go to Mississippi to visit my family, they are usually left alone and don't want to eat what my mother serves either, like the whole catfish, oxtails, greens and cornbread. I wanted to write a book about how it affects all of our lives."

It hurt me to my heart to hear him express those concerns, but I knew he was right because of what I saw with my own cousins and family members. As time has passed, here's what I would say now. If any parent is having trouble with similar scenarios, you must sit your sons down and explain to them that they are different and special. When we mix the races, we don't get a black or white, but nevertheless we get something that is beautiful and handsome. Tell them, "You are as strong, athletic, musical, talented, and gifted as anyone else. The color of your skin, the color of your eyes, or the texture of your hair does not change who you are." I advise any parent of biracial sons to not choose one culture over the other, but make sure they connect both heritages. They can choose which heritage to follow or favor when they get older. Introduce them to their relatives at an early age to keep them from feeling left out. Leave them with their uncles and aunts to learn about their family. Don't wait years before you make those visits.

## Molestation

Molestation is a nationwide epidemic that not only affects our girls, but our boys. It is unfortunate that many of our sons have had to face this demon. What is it that makes a man or woman to sexually force themselves on a child? A sexual predator is a weak-minded person and we are around weak-minded people all of the time. We must be careful where we leave our children and in whose hands we leave them. We can no longer judge a book by its cover. Weak-minded people are in all races and nationalities. They do not show their faces. You do not know who they are, but they are there. How do you fix something that is broken? We must talk about it, undergo effective counseling, and pray. How do we stop it from happening to the next person? We must talk to our sons about it at an early age. Why? The problem of child sexual abuse must be directly addressed in a responsible manner. This allows the child to have proper awareness of the subject matter, regardless of how difficult it is. It usually happens early in life. Don't wait until then to talk about it. Prepare them and alert them as though it is a fire drill at school.

## Forgiveness

I am a strong believer that forgiveness releases a lot of mental and emotional pressure. Our young sons need to know how to forgive. They can start with forgiving us, their parents, for our failures, shortcomings, and neglect. When anger and resentment is bottled up inside, it turns the soul angry and bitter. It causes people to shutdown. Forgiveness is the release valve for something someone either did or didn't do, or something they said or didn't say.

No matter how old they become, young boys never forget. They never forget the bike you promised to get for Christmas. They never forget that dog you were supposed to get for a particular birthday. They never forget that Spring Break trip you promised to take them on. They also never forget they saw you hit or curse their mom, or that they saw you drunk. They never forget you promised to be at their basketball, football, or track activities, or to take them to their first day of school. In order to get an understanding with a young boy, you must sit down face-to-face and explain to him the mindset struggle, financial difficulties, the battle you had with his mother, and the struggle you had as a young weak black man.

You must ask him to forgive you. You cannot make him do it. You can only ask him to forgive you and to give you a second chance. If he decides to give you a second chance, you must be truthful with him. Be upfront and put all of the cards on the table without any hidden agendas. Remember, if you fail at this, you might not get another chance.

## Weak Dads

I did not know there was such a thing as a weak dad when I was a boy. I found out later that some of my friends had weak dads. Let me explain my definition of weak. Even in football, I saw teammates who were good athletes, quit football and I would always wonder why their dads would let them leave the sport? I am not talking about a man who is not being a provider, but rather a dad who won't put his foot down on choices that could be life-altering. Some decisions could cause boys to become movers and shakers in society. All of our sons need a push in life in order for them to see their capabilities and potential. They need to be challenged because that opens their eyes to see what they can and cannot do for themselves and helps them maximize and gain their independence. In the Bible, there is a story that is commonly referred to as David and Goliath. Can you imagine how David felt when he defeated Goliath? What did it do for his self-esteem and his motivation? The only way he could defeat Goliath first of all, was with God's favor and help. Yet, it was prior preparation that gave him the confidence that any giant could fall. Our sons must be prepared enough to know there isn't an obstacle or challenge that can defeat them.

A weak dad will produce a weak son. Single moms must be careful if they deal with a weak dad. They do not want to be a "mamadaddy" and shoulder the burden of both being the softer parent and the aggressive parent at the same time. My mom was one of the sweetest ladies you could ever meet, but when she needed me to understand and do what needed to be done, she kicked it into another gear and turned into a "mamadaddy." She went from being sweet to a strong black woman, whose tone and body language changed dramatically and I knew she said what she meant and meant what she said.

**Spoiling Moms**

Spoiling moms makes spoil brats. That is a bad habit to break. A spoiled child is usually spoiled forever. You cannot buy love. What happens when your money runs out? You can only do the best you can and that it is all required of you. You cannot give your son everything he wants because if you try to do it and you cannot, he will get it by any means necessary. You cannot give him material things to replace his dad. You cannot give him enough dump trucks, books, clothes, Jordans, or PlayStations, and you cannot replace his dad with another man. Frankly, you must be careful when dating, period. Most young sons do not want to see their mom with any other man.

## Chapter 3

## Messages to my Sisters and Brothers

**Dear Sisters:**

Here's a small tip for you to help you understand men. Through the years, many men have been raised without a father. The Temptations had a hit song called, "Papa was a Rolling Stone" and one of the famous lines from it was, "Wherever he laid his hat was his home." Back in those days, the men were gainfully employed and when a male had money, he was considered a "man." However, times were rough. The women often made money by washing and ironing clothes and linens, cleaning, or babysitting while the men worked in factories, fields, or took other jobs. When the man got paid on Friday, he put on his jacket and hat, and strolled through town with a few dollars in his pockets. He charmed some of the prettiest women who didn't know they would most likely be one-night stands. This contributed to the breakdown in the fabric of society. I want you to understand, however, men are born kings. They are meant to be strong go-getters, full of wisdom, and providers. All a real man wants is to know you appreciate him and his children are proud of him for being a man and a provider. If you show him attention, appreciation, and love, he will take care of you the rest of his life. That does not mean he won't make mistakes or make bad decisions.

If you have a son, it is possible he wants to follow in the footsteps of his father. He wants to walk like him, talk like him, and act like him. Once again, you, as a single mother, can clothe him, put a roof over his head and show him love, but one thing you cannot do is instill in him how to be a man. There's something about the roar that belongs to the mighty lion. There is something about the voice of a grown man. It represents power, strength, and domination.

A young boy without his father or a strong father-figure, is not any different than a cell phone without the charge cord—he's powerless. I am not saying he doesn't need his mother because what she brings to a son's life is incredible. Mothers bring joy, passion, patience, and beauty. After all, you are his first girlfriend. Don't get it twisted; you all are valuable. I cannot imagine a boy growing up without a mother. Mothers are the world's most beautiful beings, inside and out. I thank God for them. Mothers will go a million miles for their sons and constantly brag on them. Even when he is doing his worst, they will say, "He is doing all right." As the blues singer, Johnny "Guitar" Watson, would say, "That's a Real Mother for You."

My mother is incredible. She never had a whole lot of money, but she had a trillion dollars worth of love. She will give you the shirt off of her back. Even after you failed her, she would still open her door and give you a second chance. When God made Erma Lee "Kitty" O'Bryant, He broke the mold. I am constantly working hard and grinding because my mom gave me wisdom, knowledge, love, understanding, and respect. I want to get in the position to give back to her. My mother doesn't ask for anything, but she deserves the world.

Once again my heart goes out to all of the single parents, especially grandparents. However, single mothers have a job to do. It will not be easy, but God will give you the strength to endure. Remember, sons do not accept other men too quickly. The timing must be right, the chemistry must be right, but it can work. I have had good men as step-fathers myself. As my grandmother, Rosa Lee O'Bryant would say, "In all thy 'gettings,' get an understanding."

Siblings, take care of one another. Be open to talk and listen. Many siblings are distant. Don't wait until you get old and sick before you look out for one another. That makes for a scary family reunion. My prayer is that God fixes this.

**Dear Brothers:**

I hear many black men say they have tried to help another black man, but he won't do right. Some say even their own brother, cousin, or best friend, won't do right. I also heard several black men say, "He thinks he knows everything and you can't tell him anything." I have encountered that many times and the reason is he thinks he is a king. That's understandable. He is born a king full of wisdom and knowledge. He doesn't take orders well, because it is in him to give orders. He is a boss king and he comes from a long lineage of kings from the continents of Africa.

The Bible says God told Noah to get two animals of every kind. Only in Africa will you find most of these animals that was on that ark: zebras, lions, tigers, elephants, giraffes, hippopotamus, gorillas, and many of different kinds of birds, monkeys, and snakes. Africa also has a history of strong black men. Men are respected in Africa.

You must work hard to be a strong black man. It is not easy to do. Most of the whole world is against the black man. We need more strong black men as leaders. Single mothers, grandmothers, aunts, uncles, family and friends, please, let's build strong black men. We need a drastic change. I call on the village because if we do not fight, we will lose the battle.

Thank you, strong black men for being you and thank you strong black women for being you. My attempt is not to step on your shoes, my goal is to polish them. A boy is born a male, but he must find his instinct in becoming a strong black man. He must be around strong men who will help him find his way. He will not get it by being around women all of the time. Iron sharpens iron. Teach one, reach one. Nothing has changed. It still takes a village to raise a strong black man. Trust me, I know. I have been there too many times. There were times I wanted to give up, but the village wouldn't let me. I thought about all of the people I would let down and the people who really loved me. I had to realize God brought me here for a reason and a purpose. It took time for me to find that out and if you ask God what your purpose is, in time, He will let you know. It could be simple. It is never too late to ask. You are never too old to know. We all have a purpose. Find your purpose.

On the way to your purpose, become a producer instead of a consumer. Blacks spend more money than any other race of people. According to a recent report by the Nielson company, Blacks in America spend $1.2 trillion annually. That must stop. The other races laugh at us behind our backs and sometime in our faces. They think we are crazy to work hard all week and spend all of our check on material things. They take our money and go back to their countries and build homes and invest in other family businesses. Families in most of all of the other races come together and discuss politics and other matters of importance and put their money together. They also appoint people in position to make it work. Black men, we built this country called America. Buy some land and get to work. Do good business. Stop buying and start selling. Let's stand up, my strong black men and women. There is much room for us.

## My Words to a Young Black man on his way to Being Strong

My young brothers across the globe, I don't know you personally, but I wrote this book because of my concern and my love for each of you. I wish that when I was young boy, I would have had a book like this to read over and over again for myself. This is only a guide. I thank God for what I had. A single parent raised me, too, and she did a wonderful job, but at the age of 52, I still deal with the lack of a father. But guess what? I made it. In my twenties, I was a young black man, and in my thirties, I was a black man. In my forties, I became a strong black man. It goes back to the old saying, "If I knew then what I know now."

If I knew then what I know now, my life might have been different. I cannot turn back time, however, I want to impress upon you, to not waste time. Time is precious and it is something that can never be regained.

I am not asking you to be a conqueror, but be more than a conqueror. I am not asking you to be a man, but be a strong black man. Your opportunity is now to maximize your life, be what you want to be, and have what you want to have. At the end of the day, I need you to not let the cycle of being a weak black man continue. Be all you can be for your children and not let them experience what might have happened to you. It starts with you.

Young men, your parents do not ask you to be a millionaire, or an athlete like Kobe Bryant, but they do want you to take care of yourself and represent them with pride. You will not win every race, and you will not hit every three-pointer, but do your best and when you walk down the street and see another young black man who may be wayward, offer him support or guidance in the same way you received it.

Therefore, after you have read this book for perhaps the second or third time, pass it on to someone else.

## **Characteristics of a Strong Black Man**

Strong but humble
Strong and respectful
Strong but with compassion
Strong and independent
Strong and full of wisdom and knowledge
Strong and trustworthy
Strong and a go-getter
Strong but loveable
Strong and understanding
So thank you, love you, God bless you!!

Words from a strong black man,
—**Marvin O'Bryant Sr.**

# Who is Marvin O'Bryant?

Marvin O'Bryant is a fifty-three-year-old black man who moved to Texas in 1989 and has since spent three decades as a barber. As someone who has owned several barber and beauty shops, Marvin says he would not trade the barber/stylist industry for anything in the world because of the knowledge and wisdom he has gained. He loves people and the beauty industry gave him the insight to learn people first hand. He has met people from various backgrounds, ranging from judges and politicians to the homeless. Most of them say the same thing, "If you ask him for a minute, he will give you five."

Most people believe Marvin never meets a stranger and has a powerful motivation to help people, mentor, build courage, and inspire others. His message is "Get up and go," and "Do it now, because nobody will do it for you." A favorite saying is, "Stay ready, so you don't have to get ready."

God has blessed Marvin to write three other books, *From Barber to Baller to Broke to Back Again, Life Without a Father,* and *No More Excuses.* He plans to release his fifth book, *I Woke up Black,* in late 2020.

Marvin and his wife, Angela, share four children. Besides writing, the emerging film and screenwriter, director, and producer, plans to get closer to God, and continue to learn how to understand people who are on different levels. He says, "I can handle a person who has nothing, but I can't handle a person who wants nothing."

www.ingramcontent.com/pod-product-compliance
Lightning Source LLC
Chambersburg PA
CBHW071036080526
44587CB00015B/2644